Skills for Better Reading
\<Basic\>

構造で読む英文エッセイ〈初級編〉

Yumiko Ishitani

NAN'UN-DO

Skills for Better Reading
\<Basic\>

Copyright©2019

Yumiko Ishitani

All rights Reserved

No part of this book may be reproduced in any form without written permission from the author and Nan'un-do Co., Ltd.

このテキストの音声を無料で視聴(ストリーミング)・ダウンロードできます。自習用音声としてご活用ください。
以下のサイトにアクセスしてテキスト番号で検索してください。

https://nanun-do.com　テキスト番号 [**511969**]

※ 無線LAN(WiFi)に接続してのご利用を推奨いたします。

※ 音声ダウンロードはZipファイルでの提供になります。お使いの機器によっては別途ソフトウェア(アプリケーション)の導入が必要となります。

Skills for Better Reading \<Basic\> 音声ダウンロードページは左記のQRコードからもご利用になれます。

1 構造で読む英文エッセイ

　本書の目的は、「全体的な構造を考えながら英文エッセイを読むこと」に慣れてもらうことにあります。少し難しい内容でも、全体的な流れがわかれば筆者の言わんとするところがわかってきます。

　英文では日本文よりも「論理性」が重要です。それぞれのパラグラフがそれぞれの役割を持っていて、その組み合わせで、論理的な流れを作り出しているのです。各パラグラフの役割がわかれば、「次にはこういう内容が来るかな？」「筆者はこういう方向に行こうとしているのかな？」という推測が可能になるはずです。

　本書では、よく使われるエッセイ構造を大きく４つに分類しています。
　　①「自分の意見を明確にして、その理由を挙げる」
　　②「例や様々な意見を列挙する」
　　③「なんらかの事象を時間的流れに従って追っていく」
　　④「違った角度からトピックの肉付けをする」

　新聞・雑誌の英文では、こうした基本的パターンをさまざまに組みわせたものが使われ、もちろんそれほど単純ではないのですが、構造の基本を身につけているかどうかでかなり理解度が変わってくるはずです。

　最後に本書作成にあたっては、Christopher Bullsmith 氏に英文チェックをお願い致しました。

2 本書の使い方

本書はそれぞれの課が4ページ構成になっています。

1 第1ページは、エッセイ構造図です。この図でその課が狙っているエッセイのおおまかな構造を理解してください。

2 第2ページは、各課がテーマとしている構成パターンを使った読みもの（Reading A）です。テーマになっている構造を頭に入れながら読んでください。まずはさっと読んで構造をつかみ、そのあと個々の英文をしっかり読み込んでください。

3 第3ページでは、Reading Aに沿った問題がつけられています。1の問題は日本語で、それぞれのパラグラフについて内容をつかんでいるかを問います。2-3の問題は全て英語にしてあります。英語に頭を切り替えて、できるだけたくさんの英語に触れてください。

4 第4ページは、もうひとつの軽い読み物、Reading Bです。こちらも、その課でテーマになっているエッセイ構造になっています。Reading Aよりも短く、簡単になっていますので、パラグラフ読みができるかどうか確認してください。

本書はあくまでも、全体的な内容をつかむということを目的にしています。細かいところを気にせずに、パラグラフのポイント、ポイントを素早くつかむということに重きを置いています。もちろんさらにReading力をつけるためには、精読することも必要ですので、あとで英文の細かな分析を行うこともお勧めします。

3 ここで扱う4つのエッセイパターン

このテキストでは、エッセイのパターンを次の4つの型に分けています。

1. 意見サポート型
2. パラグラフ並列型
3. 直線型
4. 異質パラグラフ型

エッセイの構造がどのようになっているのか以下に簡単に図示します。

◎ 第1のパターン：意見サポート型

Unit 1〜3

```
導入（意見の提示）
    ↑         ↑
理由❶      理由❷

結論（導入で述べた意見の確認）
```

最初に自分の意見を明確にし、それを支える理由をその後の段落で述べていくパターン。最後の段落では最初に述べた意見をもう一度確認します。このテキストでは、①〜③ 課で次の3種類を提示します。

① 結論・理由
② 社会事象の説明
③ 結果・原因

◎ 第2のパターン：パラグラフ並列型

Unit 4〜7

```
導入（トピックの提示）

意見A  ⇔  意見B

結び（発展など）
```

トピックを説明するいくつかのパラグラフがそれぞれ同じ重要性をもって並列に配置されるエッセイパターンです。それぞれのパラグラフは相対関係にあります。このテキストでは、④〜⑦ 課で次の4種類を提示します。

④ 複数の意見
⑤ 比較
⑥ 賛成・反対
⑦ 分類

◎ 第3のパターン：直線フロー型

時間の流れに沿って順に説明をしていくものです。このテキストでは、⑧〜⑩課で次の3種類を提示します。

⑧ 歴史
⑨ 過程
⑩ 原因ー結果

◎ 第4のパターン：異質パラグラフ型

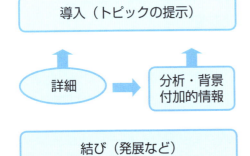

役割の違う複数のパラグラフで構成するエッセイパターンです。このテキストでは⑪〜⑭課で次の4種類を提示します。

⑪ 言葉の定義
⑫ 調査
⑬ 新製品
⑭ グラフ

Contents

Part I 第1のパターン：意見サポート型

1 Conclusion / Reasons — 11
理由で押し切る！

　A. Right-hand traffic or left-hand traffic?
　B. Should consumption tax be raised?

2 Social Trend — 15
社会事象を考える

　A. The increase of depression
　B. US birth rate is declining.

3 Result / Cause — 19
原因を究明する

　A. Casino law was passed.
　B. Why does Korea keep the draft system?

Part II 第2のパターン：パラグラフ並列型

4 Several Explanations — 25
いくつかの説明

　A. What was the cause of Napoleon's death?
　B. Springtime depression peak

5 Comparison — 29
比較してみよう！

　A. College and university
　B. A combined junior and senior high school and an ordinary high school

6 For and Against — 33
賛成と反対

　A. A married couple having different surnames
　B. School uniforms

7 Classification — 37
分類してみよう！

　A. Lies
　B. Manga

Part III　第3のパターン：直線フロー型

8　History　　　　　　　　　　　　　　　　　　　　43
歴史を知ろう！

A. Bill Gates
B. Steve Jobs

9　Process　　　　　　　　　　　　　　　　　　　　47
過程を説明する

A. How to make tempura
B. How to make "niku-jaga (meat and potatoes)"

10　Cause and Effect　　　　　　　　　　　　　　　51
原因と結果

A. Work-style reforms
B. School meals

Part IV　第4のパターン：異質パラグラフ型

11　Definition of a New Word　　　　　　　　　　57
新しい言葉を説明しよう！

A. Cool Japan
B. Crowdfunding

12　Research　　　　　　　　　　　　　　　　　　61
調査をしてみよう！

A. Self-esteem declines after retirement.
B. The more sleep, the happier

13　New Products, New Service　　　　　　　　　65
新製品・新サービス

A. A nosy coin bank
B. Gerontaxi

14　Reading Graphs　　　　　　　　　　　　　　　69
グラフを読む

A. Old people are irritated.
B. More middle-aged single people live with their parents.

Part I

第1のパターン：**意見サポート型**
（Unit 1 〜 3）

最初に自分の意見を明確にし、それを支える理由をその後の段落で述べていくパターン。最後の段落では最初に述べた意見をもう一度確認します。このテキストでは、①〜③ 課で次の3種類を提示します。

① **結論・理由**
② **社会事象の説明**
③ **結果・原因**

Part I

1 Conclusion / Reasons
理由で押し切る！

― エッセイ構成 ―

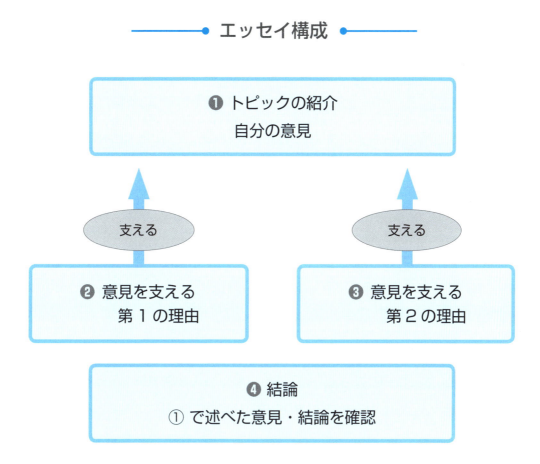

論議を呼ぶようなトピックが出されて、「賛成か」「反対か」というような議論を展開するエッセイの型です。アカデミックなエッセイのパターンとして定番です。この型ではまず最初に結論が来るので、筆者が何を目標に書いていくのかということが明確です。その後のパラグラフの役割はこの結論を裏付ける理由となります。

A Right-hand traffic or left-hand traffic?

1 Right-hand traffic (RHT) means that cars must use the right side of the road and left-hand traffic (LHT) means the opposite. In general, the former British colonies now use LHT. Japan is also an LHT country, because they introduced the traffic rules from Britain. Now, many people are driving outside their country, so such a basic traffic rule should be united to reduce accidents. So RHT or LHT? I support RHT for the following reasons.

2 The first reason is that more countries use RHT in the world. RHT is used in 163 countries, LHT in 76 countries. Originally, LHT was more common than RHT probably because many people are right-handed, but Napoleon of France chose RHT for his military strategy. He imposed this system all over Europe, but Britain didn't follow him. When America became independent from Britain, they chose RHT. As America became powerful, many countries followed her. RHT is now more common in the world, so all countries should accept RHT for traffic safety.

3 The second reason is that water traffic and air traffic both use RHT, because the USA supports it. Now that RHT is the common rule on the sea and in the air, why not on the land?

4 International traffic safety is more important than national pride. The world should consider this issue more seriously.

❶ それぞれの段落について、次の質問に答えなさい。

1. 筆者は基本的交通規則を統一すべきとしているがそれは何故か？

　_____

2. 筆者が右側通行を支持する第一の理由とは？

　_____

3. 筆者が右側通行を支持する第二の理由とは？

　_____

4. 筆者は何が最も大切であると言っているか？

　_____

❷ Choose the correct word from each pair of brackets.

The writer says that all the countries should follow (¹ RHT / LHT). The first reason is that the number of the countries which follow (² RHT / LHT) is larger than that of the countries which follow (³ RHT / LHT). Now, Britain and former British colonies follow (⁴ RHT / LHT) and the US and European countries follow (⁵ RHT / LHT). The second reason is that water traffic and air traffic follow (⁶ RHT / LHT).

❸ Which traffic system does each country follow, RHT or LHT?

1. Japan　　　(　　　　)
2. the US　　 (　　　　)
3. the UK　　 (　　　　)
4. Australia　 (　　　　)
5. France　　 (　　　　)
6. India　　　(　　　　)
7. Spain　　　(　　　　)

Notes

right-hand traffic 右側通行
1　opposite 反対　in general 一般に　former 以前の　colony 植民地
　　introduce 導入する　unite 統一する　reduce 減らす　following 次の
2　originally 元々　military 軍隊の　strategy 戦略　impose 課す　safety 安全
4　issue 問題　seriously 真剣に

B Should consumption tax be raised?

1 The Japanese government is planning to raise consumption tax from 8% to 10%. Although many people are against this idea, I support this idea for the following two reasons.

2 The first reason is that you will not lose motivation to work. If consumption tax is raised, you will work harder to buy what you want. If income tax is raised instead of consumption tax, you will lose motivation to work, because you know you will lose more money if you earn more money.

3 The second reason is that consumption tax is easier to collect and fairer than the other types of tax. In the case of income tax, people or companies may cheat. They may report false information about income, cost or sales.

4 These are the reasons why I support the raise of consumption tax, if raising tax is really necessary.

上の文章の内容をまとめてみよう。

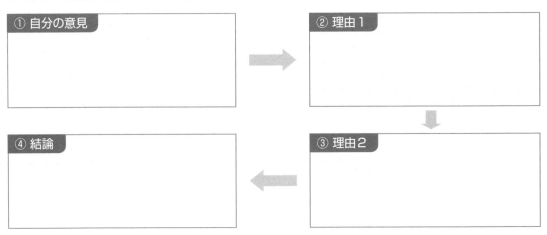

Notes
consumption tax 消費税 raise 上げる
2 motivation 動機 income tax 所得税 instead of ～の代わりに earn 稼ぐ
3 collect 集める fair 公平な in the case of ～の場合は cheat 騙す income 収入

Part I

2 Social Trend
社会事象を考える

—— エッセイ構成 ——

❶ トピックの紹介
ある社会事象の提示

支える　　　　支える

❷ 原因1
その社会事象を引き起こした第1の原因

❸ 原因2
その社会事象を引き起こした第2の原因

❹ 結論・まとめ

トピックとなる社会事象を紹介し、その事象が現れた社会的原因・背景を提示していきます。それぞれあげる原因が、トピックとなる事象を説明し、支える構成となっています。

A The increase of depression

[1]   Nowadays the number of people who suffer from depression is increasing. There are many people who can't go to school or work. Why are such people depressed?

[2]   The first reason is that many mental problems now have names. In the past, people who were depressed were regarded as lazy, or antisocial. People didn't think they were ill but thought they were lazy. However, nowadays, doctors say such people are mentally ill and the media now features many new mental illnesses.

[3]   The second reason is that people seem to be more stressed in this new society. Society is now more complicated and the traditional value system is breaking down. People are worried about how other people think of them. Computers are also a stress to many people.

[4]   Depression may be a modern illness. People have to cope with it.

❶ それぞれの段落について、次の質問に答えなさい。

1. 話題となっている社会傾向とは？

   _____

2. 第一の理由とは？

   _____

3. 第二の理由とは？

   _____

4. 筆者は鬱(うつ)をどう表現しているか？

   _____

❷ True or False questions.

1. The number of people who can't go to school or work is declining.　　(　)
2. Depressed people in the past were regarded as crazy by other people.　(　)
3. The media now talks a lot about mental illness.　　(　)
4. People seem to be more stressed in this computerized society now.　　(　)
5. There was depression in the past, too, but it was not regarded as illness.

   (　)

❸ Fill in the blanks to complete the following summary.

More people are suffering from (¹　　　　　) than in the past. Many people can't go to school or work. People thought that depressed people were not ill but (²　　　　　) in the past. Now such people are thought to be (³　　　　　) ill. And the modern society is more (⁴　　　　　), so more people find it hard to live in this modern society.

Notes

　　increase 増加　　depression 鬱(うつ)
[1] suffer from ～に苦しむ　　be depressed 憂鬱(ゆううつ)になっている
[2] mental 精神の　　regard ～とみなす　　lazy 怠惰(たいだ)な　　antisocial 非社交的な　　media メディア
　　feature ～を取り上げる　　mental illness 精神病
[3] be stressed ストレスを感じている　　complicated 複雑な
[4] value system 価値観　　break down 崩壊(ほうかい)する
[5] cope with ～に対処する

B   US birth rate is declining.

1   The decline in birth rate is a common problem in developed countries. According to new research, about 3.8 million babies were born in the US in 2017. This number is 2% lower than that of 2016, and the lowest number of births in 30 years. On the contrary, women in their early 40s showed an increase in their birth rate.

2   The main reason is employment. Even though the economic recession ended in 2009, people still feel uneasy about their economic situation.

3   In addition, single people may think they still have something to do before having kids, such as getting a college degree, having enough income or completing their dream. The increase in the birth rate of women over 40 is because they can't wait any more to have kids.

4   What will American people do to solve this problem?

上の文章の内容をまとめてみよう。

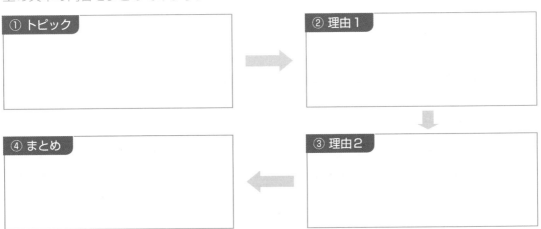

① トピック

② 理由1

③ 理由2

④ まとめ

Notes

birth rate 出生率   decline 減少する
1 common 共通の   according to ~ ~によると   research 調査   million 百万   on the contrary 対照的に
2 employment 雇用   even though ~ たとえ~であっても   recession 不況   end 終わる
   uneasy 不安な   situation 状況
3 in addition さらに   single 独身の   degree 学位   income 収入   complete 完成させる   increase 増加
4 solve 解決する

Part I

3 Result / Cause
原因を究明する

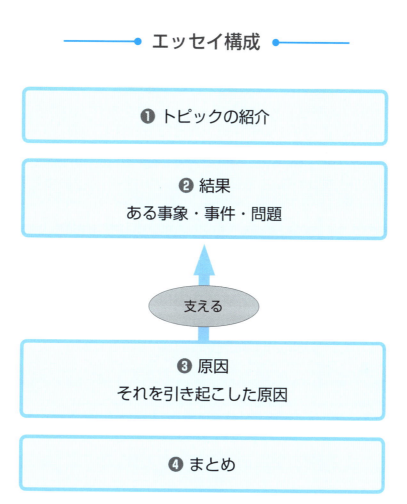

● エッセイ構成

❶ トピックの紹介

❷ 結果
ある事象・事件・問題

支える

❸ 原因
それを引き起こした原因

❹ まとめ

現在起こっている事象、最近のニュースを結果ととらえ、なぜその結果が引き起こされたのか、その原因を調べていくエッセイです。ここではカジノ法と韓国の徴兵制を取り上げ、なぜそのような結果に至ったのかという原因を第3パラグラフで述べます。

A Casino law was passed.

⑴   Generally speaking, gambling is not something Japanese people like. However, Japan has decided to accept gambling.

⑵   In 2018, "Casino Legislation" was passed in Japan. There were many opponents to this law, but the government decided to accept casinos. Why did the government decide to accept casinos?

⑶   The main reason was that the government wanted to make Japan a tourist destination and attract more tourists from foreign countries. The government recognized Japan would not be able to expect economic development in the traditional markets any more. So they were looking for a new market. Their answer was tourism. Japan started to think of developing more Integrated Resorts (IR). Casinos were a part of it. The Tokyo Olympic Games were also an important element for passing the casino law.

⑷   There are still people who are against casinos. The government has to solve many problems before casinos are built.

❶ それぞれの段落について、次の質問に答えなさい。

1. 日本人のギャンブルに対する態度とは？
   _____

2. 2018年に通された法とは何か？
   _____

3. この法を通した理由は？
   _____

4. 政府はどうしなければならないか？
   _____

❷ True or False questions.

1. There were many casinos in Japan in the past. (　)
2. In 2018, "Casino Legislation" was passed in Japan. (　)
3. The main purpose of this law is to encourage Japanese people to like gambling. (　)
4. The government is planning to build casinos as a part of IR. (　)
5. The government thought Japanese traditional markets would recover after the Tokyo Olympic Games. (　)

❸ Find the word which each statement refers to.

1. a public room or building where gambling games are played
   (　　　　　　　　　　)
2. playing games of chance for money　(　　　　　　　　　　)
3. a person who disagrees with a proposal　(　　　　　　　　　　)
4. a person who is traveling or visiting a place for pleasure
   (　　　　　　　　　　)

Notes

　　casino law カジノ法　　pass 通過させる
1　generally speaking 一般的に言って　　gambling ギャンブル
2　legislation 法　　opponent 反対者
3　a tourist destination 観光地　　attract 惹きつける　　recognize 認める　　traditional 従来の
　　tourism 観光　　Integrated Resort 統合型リゾート　　element 要素

B   Why does Korea keep the draft system?

1. After World War II, many countries have dismissed the draft system. However, there are still 64 countries which keep the draft system.

2. Korea is one of them. Korean young men between 18 and 19 years old have to take a physical check for the draft. People who passed the physical check have to enter military service for two years between 19 and 30 years old. Why does Korea have the draft system?

3. Many Asian countries became peaceful after World War II. However, the Korean War started in 1950. North Korea was supported by the USSR and China, and South Korea by the USA. The war was a part of the Cold War. In 1953, a cease-fire was agreed, but the Korean War has not yet finished. Korea needs the draft system, because the country is still at war against North Korea.

4. Even famous people such as actors and singers cannot escape the draft and their entry into military service often becomes big news.

上の文章の内容をまとめてみよう。

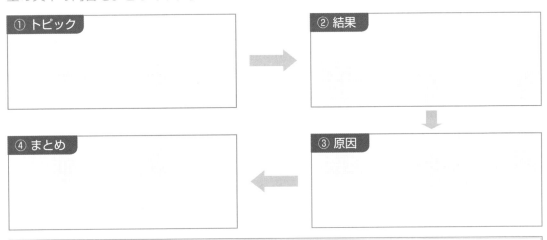

Notes

Korea 韓国　　draft 徴兵
1. dismiss 捨てる
2. physical check 身体検査・健康診断　　military service 兵役
3. the USSR ソ連　　the Cold War 冷戦　　cease-fire 休戦　　agree 同意する
4. escape 逃れる　　entry into military service 入隊

Part II

第2のパターン：パラグラフ並列型
(Unit 4 〜 7)

導入（トピックの提示）

意見 A 意見 B

結び（発展など）

トピックを説明するいくつかのパラグラフがそれぞれ同じ重要性をもって並列に配置されるエッセイパターンです。それぞれのパラグラフは相対関係にあります。このテキストでは、④〜⑦ 課で次の4種類を提示します。

④ **複数の意見**
⑤ **比較**
⑥ **賛成・反対**
⑦ **分類**

Part II

4 Several Explanations
いくつかの説明

──── エッセイ構成 ────

❶ トピックの紹介

❷ 第1の説明 ⇔対照⇔ ❸ 第2の説明 ⇔対照⇔ ❹ 第3の説明

❺ まとめ・コメント

不思議な自然現象や今だに謎に包まれている歴史的事件などを取り上げて、巷(ちまた)に流れる噂(うわさ)を紹介するものです。一つの出来事について様々な説明が紹介されます。

A What was the cause of Napoleon's death?

[1]   Napoleon Bonaparte is a hero in world history. Starting as an ordinary officer, he became the French Emperor. After he lost the war against Russia, he was sent to the island of Elba. He escaped Elba, but lost the war against Britain and was sent to the island of Saint Helena. He was there for six years and died. There have been some rumors about his death.

[2]   The first rumor is the most reliable. Napoleon died of stomach cancer. Napoleon's father had died of stomach cancer, so it was likely that Napoleon had the same disease as his father.

[3]   The second rumor is that Napoleon was poisoned and killed. According to the rumor, when he was dying, Napoleon said, "I was killed by Britain". Because Napoleon's dead body was well preserved when it reached France, some people think that he was poisoned. Arsenic prevents a dead body from decay.

[4]   The third rumor is that Napoleon was addicted to arsenic. At that time, arsenic was used in wallpaper. Napoleon had to stay in a room surrounded by such toxic wallpaper for six years, so he was addicted to the poison.

[5]   There are some other rumors, such as his kidneys were damaged because of his eating and drinking habits. The real cause of Napoleon's death is still a mystery.

❶ それぞれの段落について、次の質問に答えなさい。

1. ナポレオンが流刑になった二つの島の名前は？

　_____

2. ナポレオンの胃癌説を裏付ける事実とは？

　_____

3. ナポレオンの遺体がフランスに到着した時、どんな状態だったか？

　_____

4. ナポレオンはなぜヒ素中毒になったと言われたか？

　_____

5. そのほかの噂とは？

　_____

❷ According to the passage, which rumor is each statement linked to? Choose the answer from the box below.

1. Napoleon's dead body was well preserved for a long time. (　)
2. Napoleon was confined in a small room. (　)
3. Napoleon said he was killed by Britain. (　)
4. Napoleon's father died of stomach cancer. (　)
5. Wallpaper contained a toxic substance. (　)

> 1. Napoleon died of a disease.
> 2. Napoleon was killed.
> 3. Napoleon was addicted to poison.

❸ Find the word which each statement refers to.

1. someone who is in a position of authority in the army, navy etc. (　　　　)
2. information that is passed from one person to another, which may or may not be true (　　　　)
3. the organ inside your body where food is digested (　　　　)
4. a substance that can cause death or serious illness if you eat it, drink it etc. (　　　　)

Notes
1. ordinary 普通の　officer 将校　lose a war 戦争に負ける　escape ～から逃げる　rumor 噂
2. reliable 信頼の置ける　stomach cancer 胃癌　be likely ～することはありうる　disease 病気
3. poison 毒を盛る　preserve 保存する　arsenic ヒ素　prevent A from B AをBから防ぐ
4. be addicted to ～に中毒になっている　wallpaper 壁紙　toxic 毒性のある
5. kidney 腎臓　damage 損(そこ)なう

B Springtime depression peak

[1] You may think that people are depressed most in winter, because of the gloomy weather. However, depression reaches its peak in spring. Why? There are some explanations.

[2] The first explanation is the weather. If you are depressed in winter, you can think it's because it's winter. And you expect you will be fine in spring. However, if your depression does not disappear when spring comes, you will be more depressed.

[3] The second explanation is that you feel lonely in spring, because people are busy. If people around you are busy, you feel you are left alone.

[4] The third explanation is that your body changes in spring. In spring, there are various pollens in the air. Such pollens affect your body and your mental condition.

[5] "May sickness" is often used for the freshmen who are depressed in May. Spring may be the best and worst season in the year.

上の文章の内容をまとめてみよう。

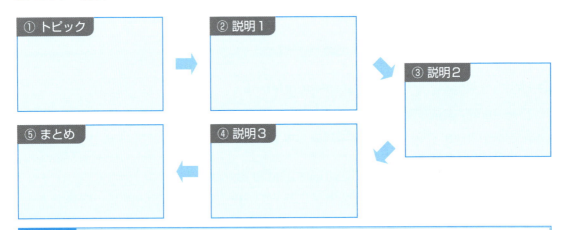

Notes

depression 鬱(う)
[1] be depressed 鬱(う)になっている   gloomy 陰鬱(いんうつ)な   reach a peak ピークに達する
[2] expect 期待する   disappear 消える
[3] lonely 寂(さび)しい   be left alone 取り残される
[4] pollen 花粉   affect 影響を与える
[5] May sickness 五月病   freshman 新入生・新入社員

Part II

5 Comparison
比較してみよう！

―――● エッセイ構成 ●―――

❶ トピックの紹介

❷ 比較対象物 A   対照 ❸ 比較対象物 B

❹ まとめ・コメント

「この二つはどう違うのだろう？」と考えたことはありませんか？このエッセイのテーマは「比較」。ここでは、比較対象物 A と B がそれぞれ別のパラグラフで述べられて両者が比較されているパターンです。

A College and University

[1] Do you know the difference between "college" and "university"? Your English teacher may say that a university is "sogo daigaku," with many faculties, and that a college is "tanka daigaku", with one or a few faculties. It's true, but their difference is more complicated.

[2] In general, a college is a smaller version of a university. Sometimes a two-year university is called a college. There is also a "community college," which is more casual than university. A community college provides a variety of subjects including non-academic subjects for local people. In the UK, a college is a smaller version of university. Several colleges make up one university. Some high schools are also called "colleges" in the UK.

[3] A university has a four-year system (three-year in the UK). In America each state has a state university and there are a lot of private universities. The size is bigger than a college and has many faculties. In the UK, a university is generally a united body of several colleges. Sometimes the colleges are quite independent, or were established before the university was. Oxford, Cambridge, University of London are all examples of this system, although many new universities don't have colleges.

[4] In this way, the difference between college and university is not clear.

❶ それぞれの段落について、次の質問に答えなさい。

1. 単科大学とはどういう大学か？

　_____

2. コミュニティカレッジとは？

　_____

3. イギリスで University と言ったらどういう形態を意味するか？

　_____

4. 結論は？

　_____

❷ True or False questions.

1. There is a clear distinction between university and college.　(　)
2. A college is a smaller version of university in many cases.　(　)
3. There are differences in the definition of college between the US and the UK.　(　)
4. Some universities are united into a college in the UK.　(　)
5. A college is more casual than a university in some cases.　(　)
6. A university has more faculties than a college in the US.　(　)

❸ Which does the following statement refer to, college or university?

1. It means a united body of some colleges in the UK.　(　　　　)
2. It has a two-year system in some cases.　(　　　　)
3. It has many faculties.　(　　　　)
4. Some high schools are called by this name in the UK.　(　　　　)
5. It sometimes provides non-academic subjects.　(　　　　)

Notes

1　faculty 学部　　complicated 複雑な
2　in general 一般に　　version 版　　casual 気軽な　　provide 供給する　　a variety of 様々な種類の
　　subject 科目　　non-academic 学術的でない　　local people 地元の人々　　make up ～を構成する
3　state 州　　establish 設立する　　example 例
4　In this way このように

B A combined junior and senior high school and an ordinary high school.

1 A combined junior and senior high school is a school in which junior high and high school are combined. How is a combined school different from an ordinary high school?

2 In a combined school, students learn with the same friends and the same teachers for six years, so their relationships become stronger and deeper. Some combined schools teach junior high school students at high school level, while ordinary junior high school students are busy preparing for high school entrance examinations.

3 In an ordinary high school, students can meet new friends at high school. They will meet students with different backgrounds and this experience will teach them many things. To pass an entrance examination to go to high school, they have to study hard. This will make them recognize the importance of efforts and make them grow up.

4 Both school types have stronger points and weaker points. Which do you choose?

上の文章の内容をまとめてみよう。

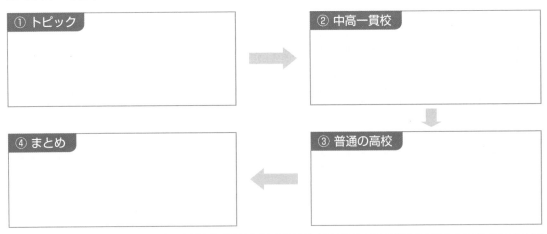

Notes
a combined junior and senior high school 中高一貫校
1 combine 合わせる　ordinary 普通の
2 be busy ～ing ～するのに忙しい　entrance examination 入試
3 background 背景　experience 経験　pass 合格する　importance 重要性　grow up 成長する
4 strong point 長所　weak point 弱点

Part II

6 For and Against
賛成と反対

── エッセイ構成 ──

❶ トピックの紹介
議論をよんでいる問題の紹介

❷ 賛成意見 対照 ❸ 反対意見

❹ まとめ・コメント

現在議論を呼んでいる問題をとりあげ、それに賛成する立場からの意見、それに反対する立場からの意見が紹介されています。Part1 の第 1 課（理由で押し切る）は、まずどちらの立場に立つかを明確にし、それを論証するものですが、本課のエッセイパターンは、自分の立場は明確にする必要はなく、客観的に賛成、反対の意見を紹介します。

A A married couple having different surnames

[1] If you are a woman, do you want to change your surname when you marry? Some people say that women should keep their surnames even after marriage. Do you agree or disagree?

[2] The supporters of this opinion say that women have the right to keep their identity. After marriage, a woman becomes a member of her husband's family. So how about her own family? To give up her surname means to give up her identity. If she has a career and has gained a good reputation under her own name, she will lose her achievements. Somebody from her elementary school may try to find her, but it will be harder if she has changed her surname. If she divorces, she will be embarrassed when she has to change her surname again. If she has children, they will be embarrassed as well.

[3] The opponents of this opinion say that a family should be united under the same surname. If the mother has a different surname, it will confuse her children and cause many troubles. People can recognize her and her children are a family if they all have the same surname.

[4] There are some countries where women don't change their surname after marriage. Which do you think is better?

❶ それぞれの段落について、次の質問に答えなさい。

1. 筆者が聞きたいこととは？

   _____

2. キャリアのある女性にとって姓を変えることの不利益は？

   _____

3. 夫婦別姓に反対する人の主な理由は？

   _____

4. 海外では？

   _____

❷ True or False questions.

1. Some countries allow women to keep their surname after marriage.   (   )
2. When you want to meet your friend from elementary school, it will be hard if she has a different surname after marriage.   (   )
3. When a woman divorces, changing her name is no trouble.   (   )
4. People are not troubled even if a mother and her children have different surnames.   (   )

❸ Find the word which each statement refers to.

1. the name you share with your family   (   )
2. something you are allowed to do or have   (   )
3. someone's name or who he is   (   )
4. something you get by your own efforts   (   )
5. to end your marriage   (   )
6. to make someone feel ashamed, nervous, or uncomfortable   (   )

Notes

1 surname 姓・苗字
2 supporter 支持者　opinion 意見　right 権利　identity アイデンティティ　give up 捨てる
　career キャリア　gain 得る　reputation 評判　achievement 業績　divorce 離婚する
　be embarrassed 困る・恥をかく
3 opponent 反対者　unite 一体化する　confuse 混乱させる　cause 引き起こす

B School uniforms

1. Do you want to wear a school uniform or your own clothes when you go to school?

2. The supporters of school uniforms think that they are economical and convenient. They're economical because you don't need to buy many clothes. They're convenient because you don't have to worry about what to wear every morning. Teachers and parents will protect you outside school if you are in school uniform.

3. The opponents of a school uniform think if you wear the same clothes as other students, you will lose your personality. The kind of clothes you wear shows your way of thinking. Another reason is that you can wear different clothes according to the weather and wash them more often and easily.

4. Now, most junior high and high schools in Japan have a school uniform, choosing the merits of a school uniform.

上の文章の内容をまとめてみよう。

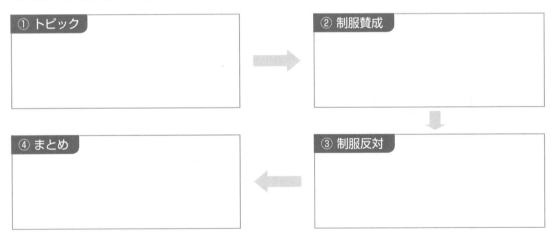

Notes
2 economical 経済的な　convenient 便利な　protect 守る
3 personality 個性　according to ～に応じて
4 merit 利点

Part II

7 Classification
分類してみよう！

エッセイ構成

❶ トピックの紹介

❷ グループA ⇔対照⇔ ❸ グループB ⇔対照⇔ ❹ グループC

❺ まとめ・コメント

ある基準を設け、その基準に従って、何かをいくつかのグループに分類します。どういう基準で分類するのかをまずはっきりさせます。それから構成要素をそれぞれのグループに振り分けていきます。ここでは「嘘の種類」と「漫画の種類」を考えてみます。

A Lies

1. Have you told a lie? Of course you have. However, what intention did you have when you told the lie? A bad intention or a good intention? There are three categories of lie according to the intention behind a lie.

2. The first category of lie is used to cheat or to hurt other people. When you want to get something from somebody, or when you want to hurt someone because you hate them, you tell a lie to that person or other people around them.

3. The second category of lie is used to protect yourself. When you have made a mistake and you want to conceal the mistake, you tell a lie. This kind of lie sometimes hurts other people.

4. The third category is used to protect other people. When you don't want to tell the truth to somebody because you think this fact will hurt them, you tell a lie. This kind of lie is sometimes called a "white lie."

5. To tell a lie is a bad thing, but sometimes it is necessary.

❶ それぞれの段落について、次の質問に答えなさい。

1. 三種類の嘘はどういう基準で分けられるか？

2. 第1のカテゴリーの嘘はどういうものか？

3. 第2のカテゴリーの嘘はどういうものか？

4. 第3のカテゴリーの嘘はどういうものか？

5. 嘘は善か悪か？

❷ True or False questions.

1. Some lies are necessary. ( )
2. Some people tell a lie when they want to hurt other people. ( )
3. Some people tell a lie when they want to protect other people. ( )
4. A "white lie" is a lie to protect yourself. ( )
5. If you tell a lie to conceal your mistake, such a lie is called a "white lie". ( )

❸ Fill in the blanks to complete the following summary.

Lies can be classified into (^{1}) categories. You tell a lie when you want to (^{2}) somebody you hate. You tell a lie when you want to conceal your (^{3}). And you tell a lie when you don't want to (^{4}) somebody. Such a lie is called a (^{5}) lie. Some lies are (^{6}).

Notes

1 lie 嘘　intention 意図　category カテゴリー　according to 〜に応じて
2 cheat 騙(だま)す　hurt 傷つける　hate 憎(にく)む
3 mistake 過(あやま)ち　conceal 隠す
4 truth 真実

B Manga

[1] Manga is now a part of Japanese culture. Manga can be classified into mainly four categories according to who are reading them.

[2] The first category is for children. A comic magazine "Korokoro Comic" is an example. Children can learn how to read, how to use their imaginations and sometimes how to behave in society.

[3] The second category is for boys. Action, adventure, friendship, sports are popular genres for boys. "Shonen Jump" is a good example.

[4] The third category is for girls. The most popular genre for girls is love romance. Sports, jobs, and heart-warming stories are also popular genres. "Hana to Yume" is an example.

[5] The fourth category of manga is for education. History manga is the most popular. Many high school students read "Asaki Yumemishi," a manga story of a Japanese classic, "Tale of Genji."

[6] Manga are now largely read online rather than in the form of paper magazines, but they are still popular among people.

上の文章の内容をまとめてみよう。

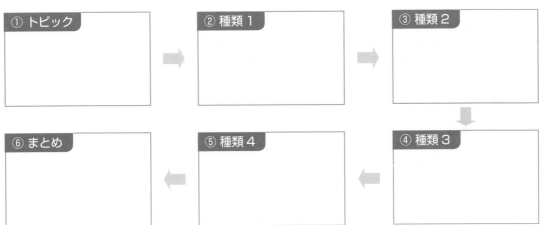

Notes

[1] classify 分類する　　[2] imagination 想像力　　behave 振る舞う
[3] adventure 冒険　genre ジャンル　　[4] heart-warming 心温まる
[5] education 教育　classic 古典　　[6] largely 広く　online ネットで　in the form of 〜の形態で

Part III

第3のパターン：直線フロー型
（Unit 8 〜 10）

導入（トピックの提示）

↓

第1段階

↓

第2段階

↓

第3段階

まとめ・これからの発展など

時間の流れに沿って順に説明をしていくものです。このテキストでは、⑧〜⑩課で次の3種類を提示します。

⑧ 歴史
⑨ 過程
⑩ 原因―結果

Part III

8 History
歴史を知ろう！

エッセイ構成

❶ トピックの紹介

❷ 第1段階 → フロー → ❸ 第2段階 → フロー → ❹ 第3段階

❺ まとめ・コメント

この課では、あるトピックについてその時間的変遷を追っていきます。最終段階として、現在の状態、状況でまとめます。ここではビル・ゲイツとスティーブ・ジョブズのの人生を時間に沿ってたどっていきます。

A Bill Gates

[1]   Bill Gates is very famous in the IT world, and he is one of the richest men in the world.

[2]   Bill Gates was born in Seattle in 1955. He entered Harvard University in 1973 but left Harvard to make software. His dream was to make a personal computer which was not so expensive and easy to use. Bill Gates started a company called Microsoft with his friend Paul Allen.

[3]   Microsoft developed some new software, "Windows" and it was a big success. Bill Gates became one of the richest men in the world.

[4]   In 1994 Bill Gates married Melinda, who was working under him. When they traveled to Africa, they found many poor people and they wanted to save them.

[5]   In 2006, Bill Gates quit Microsoft. He wanted to focus on charity work with his wife. They started the Bill and Melinda Gates Foundation for charity. Although they have three children, they are planning to spend most of their money on charity.

[6]   Bill Gates is a successful engineer and businessman, and at the same time a philanthropist.

❶ それぞれの段落について、次の質問に答えなさい。

1. Bill Gates を簡単に説明せよ。
   _____

2. Bill Gates の学生時代の夢は？
   _____

3. Bill Gates はどうやってお金持ちになったか？
   _____

4. Gates 夫妻がアフリカ旅行で体験したこととは？
   _____

5. Bill Gates はなぜ Microsoft 社をやめたか？
   _____

6. Bill Gates はどういう人か？
   _____

❷ True or False questions.

1. Bill Gates' dream in his youth was to save poor people in Africa.　　　(　)
2. Bill Gates quit Microsoft to start a new business.　　　(　)
3. Melinda Gates didn't want Bill Gates to quit Microsoft, so Bill changed his mind.　　　(　)
4. Mr. and Mrs. Gates have been working together to help poor people.　　　(　)
5. Mr. and Mrs. Gates are planning to give most of their money to charity, although they have three children.　　　(　)
6. Bill Gates graduated from Harvard University.　　　(　)
7. Melinda Gates was working for Microsoft before she married.　　　(　)

❸ Find the word which each statement refers to.

1. the sets of programs that tell a computer how to do a particular job
   (　　　　)
2. to leave a job, school etc. without finishing it completely　　(　　　　)
3. an organization that gives money to be used for special purposes, especially for charity or research　　(　　　　)
4. a rich person who gives a lot of money to help poor people　　(　　　　)

Notes
2 enter ～に入学する
3 develop 開発する　success 成功
4 marry ～と結婚する　save 救う
5 quit 辞める　focus on ～に集中する　foundation 基金
6 successful 成功した　engineer 技術者　philanthropist 博愛主義者

B Steve Jobs

[1]   Steve Jobs is famous along with Bill Gates in the IT world. The rival story of Apple vs. Microsoft is very famous.

[2]   Steve Jobs was born in 1955 (the same year as Bill Gates was born) in San Francisco. Jobs went to Reed College for a short time and dropped out.

[3]   He started a computer company called "Apple" with his friend, Steve Wozniak. He wanted to make the personal computer easy to use, so he invented icons on the screen.

[4]   In 1985, Jobs was fired by Apple. He started NeXT, another computer company. Apple bought NeXT in 1997 and Jobs returned to Apple as CEO.

[5]   In 2011, Jobs retired as CEO of Apple and gave his position to Tim Cook. As for his private life, Jobs had a daughter from one partner (they were not married), a son and a daughter from his wife, and an adopted daughter. He died of pancreatic cancer in 2011 in California.

上の文章の内容をまとめてみよう。

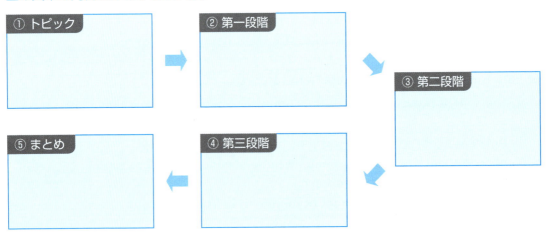

Notes
[1] along with ～と並んで   rival ライバルの   [2] drop out 中退する
[3] invent 発明する   icon アイコン   [4] fire 解雇する
[5] retire 引退する   CEO 重役   as for ～に関しては   private 私的な   partner 交際相手
    adopted daughter 養女   pancreatic cancer 膵臓癌(すいぞうがん)

Part III

9 Process
過程を説明する

―――● エッセイ構成 ●―――

❶ トピックの紹介

❷ 第1手順 —フロー→ ❸ 第2手順 —フロー→ ❹ 第3手順

❻ まとめ・コメント

何かの過程を説明する。「始めに→次に→それから→最後に」と進んでいくエッセイパターンです。ここでは簡単な料理の調理法の手順を時間軸に沿って述べていきます。トピックは「天ぷら」と「肉じゃが」です。

>> 47

A   How to make tempura

1   Tempura is a Japanese national food. This is the recipe to make tempura.

2   Cut vegetables (onion, sweet potato, eggplant, green pepper etc.), squid, shrimp and fish. Before cooking, you should keep all the ingredients in a refrigerator.

3   Put tempura flour into a bowl and add water. This mixture is called "batter." Take the ingredients from the refrigerator and dry them with kitchen paper. Dip the ingredients into the batter.

4   Heat the oil to 160-170 degrees. If you don't have a thermometer, drop a piece of batter into the oil. If the oil is hot enough, the batter will drop to the bottom and quickly come back to the top of the oil.

5   When the oil is ready, pour the battered ingredients into the hot oil. Wait until the batter is golden brown. Catch the fried tempura with chopsticks, and put it on a kitchen towel.

6   Prepare the sauce. Put and heat the broth, soy sauce and mirin in a pan and mix gently until they boil.

7   Dip tempura into the sauce, sometimes with grated radish. Instead of the sauce, you can use salt or matcha powder.

❶ それぞれの段落について、次の質問に答えなさい。

1. てんぷらはどんな料理か？
　_____

2. 切った材料を調理前にどうしろと言っているか？
　_____

3. batter とは何か？
　_____

4. 油が適温かどうか見るのに温度計がない場合どうするか？
　_____

5. てんぷらを油からとりあげる目安は？
　_____

6. てんぷらつゆの作り方は？
　_____

7. てんぷらつゆに何をつけあわせるか？
　_____

❷ Is each instruction correct? Answer with "Yes" or "No".

1. Keep the battered ingredients in the refrigerator.　　　　(Yes / No)
2. Dry the ingredients and dip them into the batter.　　　　(Yes / No)
3. Put the ingredients in the cold oil and heat the oil.　　　(Yes / No)
4. Add salt into the sauce before you eat tempura.　　　　(Yes / No)
5. Drop a piece of butter into the oil, if the butter melts, the oil is ready.
　　　　　　　　　　　　　　　　　　　　　　　　　　　(Yes / No)

❸ Put the following statements in order.

1. Pour the battered ingredients into the hot oil.
2. Cut the ingredients.
3. Dip fried ingredients into the sauce before you eat.
4. Dip the ingredients into the batter.
5. Put the ingredients into the refrigerator.
6. Heat the oil.
7. Mix tempura flour and water.

(　) → (　) → (　) → (　) → (　) → (　) → (　)

Notes

1 recipe 調理法　　2 sweet potato さつまいも　　eggplant ナス　　green pepper ピーマン
squid いか　　ingredient 材料　　refrigerator 冷蔵庫　　3 flour 粉　　bowl ボウル　　mixture 混ぜたもの
batter ころも　　dip 浸す　　4 thermometer 温度計　　5 ready 準備のできた　　pour 流し込む
battered ころもをつけた　　chopstick 箸　　6 prepare 準備する　　sauce つけ汁　　broth だし
soy sauce 醤油　　golden brown きつね色　　pan 鍋　　7 grated radish 大根おろし
instead of ～の代わりに　　matcha powder 抹茶（まっちゃ）パウダー

B How to make "niku-jaga (meat and potatoes)"

19

1 Niku-jaga means "meat and potatoes." This dish is often said to be a "taste of mother's home cooking" meal. This is the recipe to make niku-jaga.

2 Cut some potatoes, the onion and the carrot and meat into pieces. Cook shirataki noodles in the boiling water for one minute and cut them in half.

3 In a large pot, heat oil on medium heat and sauté the onion. Add the meat and cook until it becomes brown. Add the potatoes, carrots, and shirataki noodles. Add broth and seasonings (mirin, soy sauce, sake, and sugar) and boil it.

4 When it boils, turn down the heat. Put an otoshibuta (a small lid, a sheet of kitchen paper, or a piece of aluminum foil) on it and simmer for 10-15 minutes.

5 Turn off the heat. Remove the otoshibuta. Now you can eat it!

上の文章の内容をまとめてみよう。

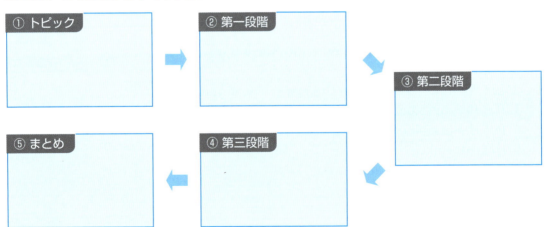

Notes
1 dish 料理　taste of mother's home cooking お袋の味
2 boiling water 沸騰(ふっとう)しているお湯　in half 半分に
3 medium heat 中火　sauté 少量の油で炒(いた)める　add 加える　broth だし　seasoning 調味料
4 turn down 弱める　lid 蓋(ふた)　aluminum foil アルミホイル　simmer とろ火で煮る
5 remove 取り除く

Part III

10 Cause & Effect
原因と結果

• エッセイ構成 •

❶ トピックの紹介

❷ 原因 フロー ❸ 結果

❹ まとめ・コメント

ボディとなるパラグラフが、原因→その結果、と進むエッセイパターン。何かの事象があり、それが原因となってあることが起こる、その過程を説明するものです。ここでは「働き方改革」と「給食」をテーマとして扱います。

A Work-style reforms

[1] "Work-style reforms" was the center of the policies promoted by Prime Minister Shinzo Abe.

[2] This policy aims at the reduction of working hours and the "equal work, equal pay" system. People will be paid on the basis of their performance rather than working hours.

[3] The government thinks work-style reforms will be a solution to many economic problems. By reducing working hours, the government thinks they can give more work chances to women, old people and irregular workers. Now, irregular workers, such as part-timers and term-contract workers account for 40% of all workers. If their wage is raised, they will buy more. As a result, the Japanese economy will improve.

[4] Japanese people have believed that to work hard is good. Work-style reforms may change their attitude toward work.

❶ それぞれの段落について、次の質問に答えなさい。

1.「働き方改革」は誰によって推進されてきたか？

_____

2. この改革では人々のお給料はどのように支払われるか？

_____

3. 労働時間を短くすることによってどういうメリットがあるか？

_____

4. これまでの日本人の労働観とは？

_____

❷ Will the following be the results of the work-style reforms? Write Y for yes and N for no.

1. People will work longer and earn more.　　　　　　　　　　(　　)
2. People will be given more equal chances to work.　　　　　(　　)
3. People will quit their job more easily.　　　　　　　　　　　(　　)
4. Women will do easier work than now.　　　　　　　　　　　(　　)
5. The wages will be more equal among people.　　　　　　　(　　)
6. Old people will have more work chances.　　　　　　　　　(　　)
7. People will buy more.　　　　　　　　　　　　　　　　　　(　　)

❸ Fill in the blanks to complete the following summary.

"Work-style reforms" will change Japanese people's (¹　　　　　　) toward work. People will be given more equal work chances to solve the current social problems. Irregular workers account for (²　　　　　　)% of all workers in Japan now. If such people are paid more, they will (³　　　　　　) more things, which will improve the Japanese (⁴　　　　　　).

Notes
1. work-style reforms 働き方改革　　policy 政策　　promote 推進する　　Prime Minister 首相
2. aim 狙う　　reduction 削減　　equal 同一の　　on the basis of ～を基礎として　　performance 業績
3. solution 解決　　reduce 減らす　　irregular worker 非正規労働者　　part-timer アルバイト
    term-contract worker 契約労働者　　account for ～を占める　　wage 賃金　　raise 上げる
    as a result その結果　　improve 進歩する
4. attitude 態度　　toward ～に対して

B School meals

1 We take school lunches for granted. School lunches have changed our lifestyle.

2 After World War II, the Japanese government started school lunches in urban areas. It was because there was not enough food for hungry children. In 1952, school lunches were extended to all elementary schools in Japan.

3 The school lunches after the War included bread and skimmed milk. These were provided by the U.S. Such Westernized school meals changed the Japanese traditional diet into a Western style diet. Many people started to eat bread, scrambled egg, salad and coffee for breakfast. Some people think the US intentionally provided such food because they wanted a new market for their agricultural products.

4 The Japanese diet has been Westernized due to the introduction of school meals.

上の文章の内容をまとめてみよう。

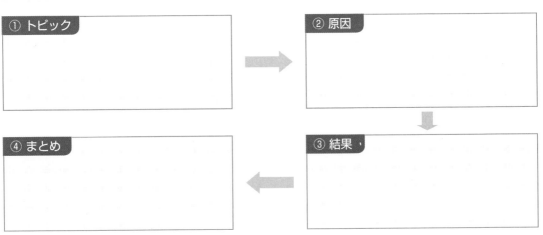

Notes

school meal 給食
1 take ~ for granted ~を当然と思う
2 urban 都市の   extend 広げる
3 include 含む   skimmed milk 脱脂粉乳   provide 供給する   Westernized 西欧化された
  traditional 伝統的な   diet 食生活   intentionally 意図的に   agricultural product 農産物
4 due to ~のせいで

Part IV

第4のパターン：**異質パラグラフ型**
（Unit 11 ～ 14）

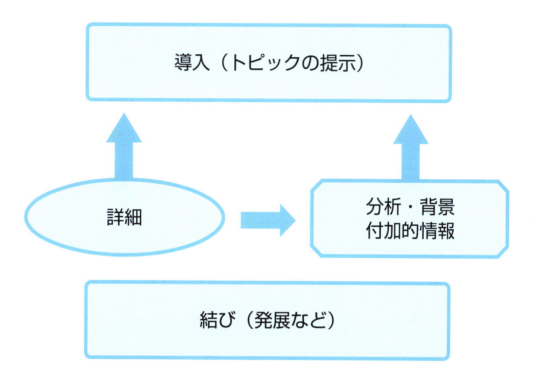

役割の違う複数のパラグラフで構成するエッセイパターンです。このテキストでは ⑪～⑭ 課で次の4種類を提示します。
⑪ **言葉の定義**
⑫ **調査**
⑬ **新製品**
⑭ **グラフ**

Part IV

11 Definition of a New Word
新しい言葉を説明しよう！

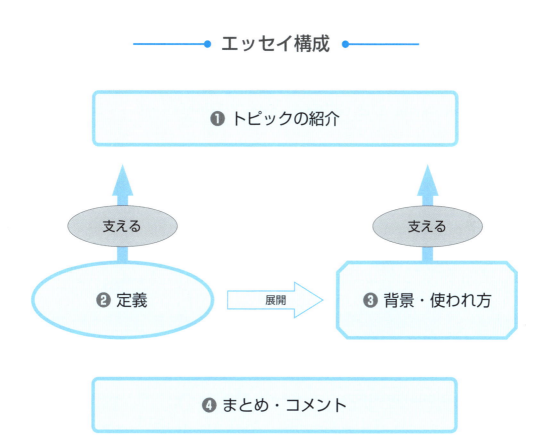

エッセイ構成

❶ トピックの紹介

支える　　　　　　　支える

❷ 定義　→展開→　❸ 背景・使われ方

❹ まとめ・コメント

テレビ・雑誌・新聞などで最近よく聞く・見る言葉をテーマにしたエッセイを紹介します。

A Cool Japan

[1]   If you hear the phrase "Cool Japan," you may think of Japanese animation or games. Do you know what "Cool Japan" really is?

[2]   In the 1990s, the UK made the phrase "Cool Britannia" in order to sell their products and culture as a national brand. It is a kind of soft power, which means a nation's cultural power which attracts other people. This brand power can help sell national products and can give economic and political power to the nation. "Cool Japan" was a copy of this "Cool Britannia."

[3]   In 2010, Japan's Ministry of Economy, Trade and Industry established a "Cool Japan Section" and started a new project. The purpose of this project was to create a new market, because Japan's traditional markets were declining. The new market involved movies, music, manga, animations, dramas, games etc. Most of them are Japan's young people's subculture.

[4]   Japan became an economic power by selling technological products in the past and now it sells cultural products as well as those traditional products.

❶ それぞれの段落について、次の質問に答えなさい。

1. Cool Japan というと何を思い浮かべるか？

   _____

2. Cool Britannia の目的とは？

   _____

3. 経産省が Cool Japan 政策を進めた経済的背景は？

   _____

4. 日本が販売する製品の変化とは？

   _____

❷ Fill in the blanks and complete the following summary.

"Cool Japan" is a phrase which is a (¹   ) of "Cool Britannia" from the 1990s. The "Cool Britannia" project aimed at selling their (²   ) products as their national (³   ). "Cool Japan" was promoted in 2010 and its purpose was to create a new (⁴   ) to make up for the declining traditional markets. The new market is based on Japanese young people's (⁵   ).

❸ Find the word which each statement refers to.

1. A type of product made by a particular company, that has a particular name or design   (   )
2. a place where people sell or buy things   (   )
3. the behavior, beliefs, and activities of a particular group of people
                                                       (   )
4. a substance that is produced for sale   (   )
5. to start a company, an organization, or a system   (   )

Notes
1. phrase 用語
2. product 製品　a national brand 国家ブランド　attract 魅了(みりょう)する　political 政治の
3. Ministry of Economy, Trade and Industry 経済貿易産業省　establish 設立する　purpose 目的　decline 衰(おとろ)える　involve 含む　subculture サブカルチャー
4. technological 技術の

B Crowdfunding

1 If you have a good idea for a product or service, but you don't have money to start a business, what would you do? You need investors. Now you can find them on the Internet. It is called "crowdfunding."

2 Crowdfunding is the use of money from many people through social media to start a new business. "Crowd" means, of course, "many people," and "funding" means "to provide money for some purpose."

3 Crowdfunding gives people the chance to raise money from anyone. A crowdfunding website provides a forum to show your idea to waiting investors. Investors can select from hundreds of projects and invest as little as $10. Investors can get money if the idea is successful.

4 If you have an idea, it may be a good chance to make money!

上の文章の内容をまとめてみよう。

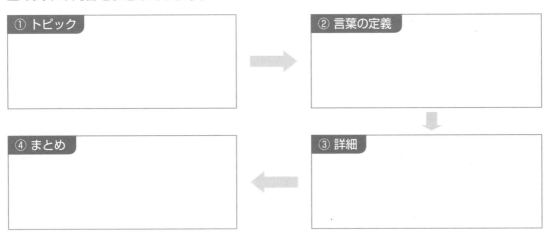

Notes
1 investor 投資家
2 provide 供給する
3 raise 集める　forum ネットワーク上の会議室　invest 投資する　as little as わずか〜の
4 make money 稼ぐ

Part IV

12 Research
調査をしてみよう！

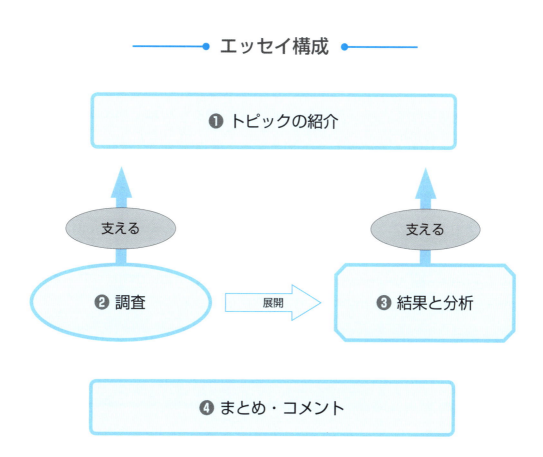

何らかの調査を提示し、その調査方法や調査結果を分析したりするパターンです。

A Self-esteem declines after retirement.

[1] The older you become, the harder your life becomes.

[2] In 2010, Live Science published some research on old people's self-esteem. The study involved 3617 American men and women from 25 to 104 years old. The participants were asked questions four times between 1986 and 2002.

[3] Self-esteem was lowest among young adults, but increased throughout adulthood, peaking at age 60, and after that it started to decline. Middle-age is people's golden time in work, family life and money. People have power and status, which raises feelings of self-esteem. In contrast, older adults have low self-esteem. This is because they experience a change in roles in society and family. For example, an empty nest, retirement and declining health. Women have lower self-esteem than men in general, but their self-esteem becomes higher than men's in their 80s and 90s.

[4] You should forget your golden age and should start a new life after retirement.

❶ それぞれの段落について、次の質問に答えなさい。

1. 年をとるにつれてどうなると言っているか？

   _____

2. Live Science が行った調査は何を調べるためのものか？

   _____

3. 老人になると自尊心が低くなるのはなぜか？

   _____

4. 定年退職後はどうするべきかと言っているか？

   _____

❷ True or False questions.

1. The participants in this research were between 25 and 104 years old. ( )
2. The participants were asked to do regular exercises every day. ( )
3. The participants answered the questions four times. ( )
4. Self-esteem was highest when the participants were young. ( )
5. Self-esteem is low when the participants are old. ( )
6. Declining health is also one reason for the low self-esteem of old people. ( )

❸ Find the word which each statement refers to.

1. confidence in your own worth or abilities   (   )
2. a person who takes part in something   (   )
3. the action of leaving your job   (   )
4. a position in the society or in a group   (   )

Notes

self-esteem 自尊心　decline 下がる　retirement 退職
② publish 公表する　research 調査　involve 含む　participant 被験者
③ adulthood 成人期　peak 頂点に達する　middle-age 中年　status 地位　raise 上げる
in contrast 反対に　experience 経験する　role 役割　empty nest 子供が巣立った後の家庭
in general 一般に

B The more sleep, the happier

1 Happiness and a good night's sleep seem to be linked, a new research suggests. The survey of more than 7,000 U.S. adults showed that people who got more sleep had a higher feeling of happiness than those got less sleep.

2 The researchers calculated the happiness scores based on participants' answers to questions about their social relationships, financial condition, and physical health.

3 The average happiness score for people who got 8 hours of sleep a night was 65.7 out of 100, 64.2 for those who got 7 hours of sleep and 59.4 for those who got 6 hours of sleep. This shows that the longer you sleep, the happier you feel.

4 If you feel you are not happy, sleep!

上の文章の内容をまとめてみよう。

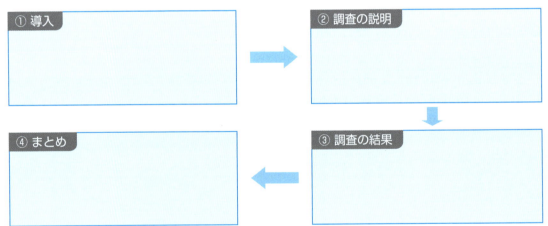

Notes
1 suggest 示唆(しさ)する   survey 調査
2 calculate 計算する   financial 経済的な   physical 身体的な

Part IV

13 New Products, New Service
新製品・新サービス

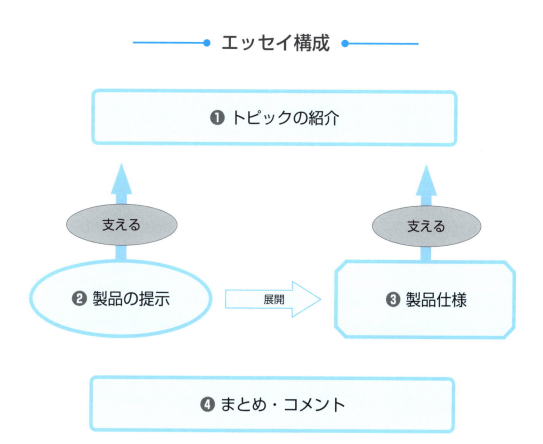

新しい製品のプロモーション・エッセイです。まずその製品の詳細や使い方を説明し、長所をアピールします。その後でその商品の価格や大きさ、色などの製品仕様が述べられます。

A A nosy coin bank

1 If you want to save money, you should have these dog's head-shaped and cat's head-shaped coin banks.

2 Takara Tommy announced a new coin bank as their new product. This bank speaks! When you put coins into this bank, it tells you how much you have put in it, and at the same time, it moves its eyes, ears, mouth and nose. When it is in a Wi-Fi environment, it tells you news and the weather forecast. If you press the button on the head, you can talk with it in simple words. This bank has a sensor and responds to the movement of people. When you pass the bank, it speaks to you. It loves jokes and negative comments: "A bank can't wait," "You haven't saved any money for three days," "Love lasts as long as you have money." These are just examples. The bank remembers 400 phrases.

3 There are two types of bank. One is only for 100 yen coins and this is named "Bank Wan" and the other is only for 500 yen coins and this is named "Bank Nyan." Bank Wan is shaped like a dog's head, and Bank Nyan is shaped like a cat's head. Each is 15cm wide, 13cm high and 13cm deep and it needs four AA batteries. The price is 9800 yen.

4 If you like to be scolded, why don't you have this bank?

❶ それぞれの段落について、次の質問に答えなさい。

1. この貯金箱の2つの種類とは？
    1. _____
    2. _____

2. この貯金箱のネガティヴなコメントの例を3つ、日本語で答えなさい。
    1. _____
    2. _____
    3. _____

3. この貯金箱の2つの種類の違いは？
    1. _____
    2. _____

4. どういう人がこの貯金箱を買ったらいいと言ってますか？
    _____

❷ True or False questions.

1. Bank Wan is only for 100 yen coins. (　)
2. Bank Nyan is for both 100 yen coins and 500 yen coins. (　)
3. Each bank needs two AA batteries. (　)
4. Each bank can be connected to Wi-Fi. (　)
5. You can talk with this bank. (　)
6. This bank can move its tongue. (　)
7. This bank will speak to you when you pass it. (　)
8. This bank responds to people's smell. (　)
9. This bank encourages you to save money by using negative comments. (　)
10. This bank costs less than 9000 yen. (　)

❸ Find the word which each statement refers to.

1. a flat, typically round piece of metal used as money　(　　　　)
2. a prediction of future events, especially coming weather　(　　　　)
3. something which examines what something is　(　　　　)

Notes

nosy おせっかいな　　a coin bank 貯金箱
1 save 貯める　　dog's head-shaped 犬の頭の形をした
2 announce 発表する　　environment 環境　　weather forecast 天気予報　　sensor センサー・感知器
   respond 反応する　　movement 動き　　pass 通り過ぎる　　negative comment 否定的なコメント
   last 持続する　　as long as 〜する限り　　phrase 言い回し
3 AA battery 単三電池
4 scold 叱(しか)る

B Gerontaxi

[1]　JTB, a tourist company, announced a new service.

[2]　JTB is planning a one-month free taxi service for old people over 70. The service is named "Gerontaxi". The target of this service is old people, who need a car to go shopping or to go to hospital, but can't drive.

[3]　The details of this service are as follows. Choose two places; a shop, a station, or a hospital. If you pay 28000 yen a month, you can use a taxi for free to go to those two places. If one of them is outside the basic zone, you must pay more. What you should do is to call the call center when you need the service.

[4]　JTB is planning to expand this business, if they can find a local taxi company which will cooperate with JTB.

上の文章の内容をまとめてみよう。

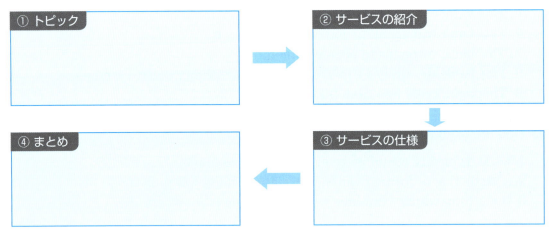

Notes
[1] announce 発表する
[2] free 無料の　　target 標的・対象
[3] detail 詳細　　as follows 次の通りである　　for free 無料で　　zone 地帯
[4] expand 拡大する　　cooperate with ～と協力する

Part IV

14 Reading Graphs
グラフを読む

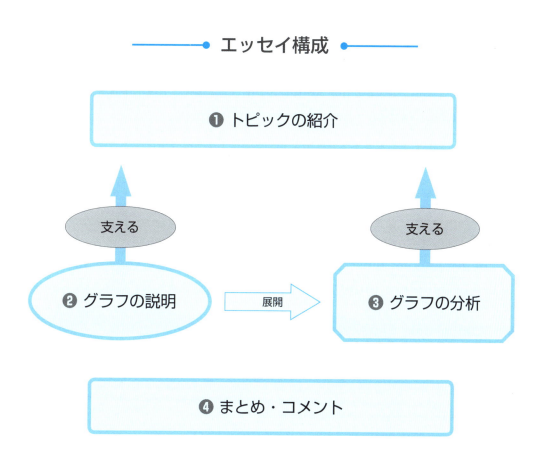

――― エッセイ構成 ―――

❶ トピックの紹介

　　支える　　　　　　　　　支える

❷ グラフの説明　　展開　　❸ グラフの分析

❹ まとめ・コメント

グラフ付きのエッセイです。グラフが何を表すものなのか、その変化の背景や分析のパラグラフが次に続きます。

>> 69

■ Reading A

A Old people are irritated.

[1]   This graph shows the number of old people over 65 who were arrested for violence.

[2]   According to this graph, it is clear that the number of violent old people has been increasing. The number in 2015 is 49 times as large as that of 1995. They use violence in stations, hospitals and other public places. Violence includes verbal violence.

[3]   Why are old people becoming more and more violent? The main reason is the number of old people has been increasing. The second reason is that their brains don't work properly and can't control their emotions. The third reason is that they are frustrated but have nobody to talk with at home. After retirement, old people lose confidence and get frustrated. If they have families, they can release their frustration by talking with them.

[4]   Old people can't recognize why they are irritated. If they recognize the reason, it may reduce their stress.

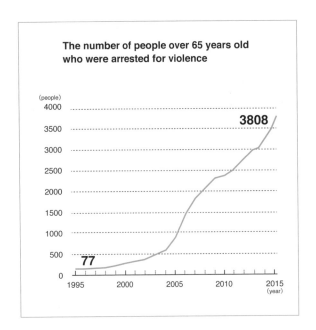

❶ それぞれの段落について、次の質問に答えなさい。

1. このグラフが表しているものとは？
   _____

2. このグラフからわかることは？
   _____

3. 暴力を振る老人が増えている理由を３つ書きなさい。
   1. _____
   2. _____
   3. _____

4. 老人のストレスを減少させるためには何をすべきと言っていますか？
   _____

❷ True or False questions.

1. Old people now use more violence than before. (　)
2. Old people don't use violence in hospitals. (　)
3. Violence can include words, too. (　)
4. Old people show a decline in brain function and can't control emotions. (　)
5. After retirement, old people become calm. (　)

❸ Fill in the blanks to complete the following summary.

This graph shows the number of (¹　　　　　) old people is (²　　　　　). This is because there is an (³　　　　　) in the number of old people. Another reason is they can't (⁴　　　　　) their emotions because of declining (⁵　　　　　) function. The other reason is they can't release their (⁶　　　　　) because they live alone.

Notes

be irritated イライラしている
1 arrest 逮捕する　violence 暴力
2 include 含む　verbal 言葉による
3 properly 適切に　emotion 感情　be frustrated 欲求不満である　retirement 引退・定年退職
   confidence 自信　release 発散させる　frustration 欲求不満・フラストレーション
4 recognize 認識する　reduce 減少させる

B More middle-aged single people live with their parents.

1 This graph shows the number of single people between 35 and 44 who still live with their parents.

2 According to this graph, the number of middle-aged people who are not married and live with their parents has been increasing. The number increased from 1 million in 1980 to 3 million in 2014.

3 Why is the number increasing? The main reason is their economic situation. When they finished university, it was quite hard to find a job. Many of them have stayed as part-timers. The words "freeter" and "NEET" were created for such people. Another reason is that the number of people who can't socialize has been increasing. The word "hikikomori" was for such people.

4 Of course there are many people who just choose to live with their parents for some reason, so the reasons may not be so simple.

上の文章の内容をまとめてみよう。

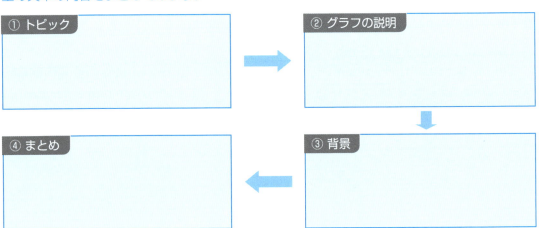

Notes

middle-aged 中年の　　single 独身の
2 million 百万
3 situation 状況　　part-timer アルバイト　　socialize 社会化する

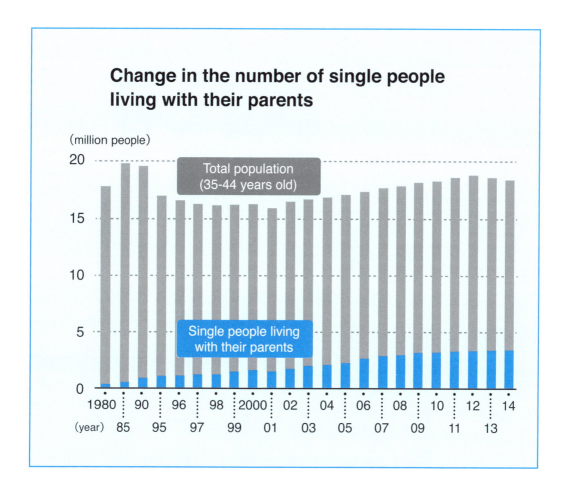

参照文献

14. Reading Graph

A. Old people are irritated.
   https://news.yahoo.co.jp/feature/511

B. More middle-aged bachelors live with their parents.
   https://news.yahoo.co.jp/feature/105

| 著作権法上、無断複写・複製は禁じられています。 |

Skills for Better Reading <Basic> [B-881]
構文で読む英文エッセイ〈初級編〉

1	刷	2019年4月1日
4	刷	2023年4月6日

著 者	石谷 由美子　　　　Yumiko Ishitani

発行者	南雲一範　Kazunori Nagumo
発行所	株式会社　南雲堂
	〒162-0801　東京都新宿区山吹町361
	NAN'UN-DO Publishing Co., Ltd.
	361 Yamabuki-cho, Shinjuku-ku, Tokyo 162-0801, Japan
	振替口座: 00160-0-46863
	TEL:　03-3268-2311（営業部：学校関係）
	03-3268-2384（営業部：書店関係）
	03-3268-2387（編集部）
	FAX:　03-3269-2486

編集者	加藤　敦
装　丁	Nスタジオ
組　版	Office haru
検　印	省　略
コード	ISBN978-4-523-17881-1 C0082

Printed in Japan

E-mail　nanundo@post.email.ne.jp
URL　https://www.nanun-do.co.jp/